Rosalie Ajzensztejn

PACIFIC
L E A R N I N G

© 2004 **Pacific Learning**
© 2002 Written by **Rosalie Ajzensztejn**
Photography: p. 1 Buzz Pictures; p. 3 Buzz Pictures; p. 4 Buzz Pictures; p. 7 Corbis/Chris Trotman (top), Buzz Pictures (bottom); p. 8 Buzz Pictures; p. 10 Corbis/Lester V. Bergman; p. 11 Buzz Pictures; p. 12 Buzz Pictures (both); p. 14 Photodisc/Chase Jarvis; p. 15 Allsport USA/Mike Powell; p. 16-17 Buzz Pictures (both); p. 18 Buzz Pictures; p. 19 Corbis/Douglas Peebles (top), Buzz Pictures (bottom); p. 20 Buzz Pictures; p. 21 Buzz Pictures; p. 23 Buzz Pictures; p. 24 Photodisc/Karl Weatherly; p. 25 Corbis; p. 30 Mary Evans/Arthur Rackham Collection; Front cover photograph by Photodisc/Karl Weatherly; back cover by Buzz Pictures
Illustrated by David Russell and Martin Ursell
U.S. edit by **Rebecca McEwen**

This Americanized Edition of *Extreme Sports,* originally published in England in 2002, is published by arrangement with Oxford University Press.

13 12 11 10
10 9 8 7 6 5 4 3 2

Published by
Pacific Learning
P.O. Box 2723
Huntington Beach, CA 92647-0723
www.pacificlearning.com

ISBN: 978-1-59055-462-3
PL-7621

Printed in China through Colorcraft Ltd., Hong Kong

PO#1122 8/10

Contents

Street Luging

Street luging is a high-speed, dangerous sport that is performed on hills. It is well suited to the warm, dry climate and smooth, fast, and hilly terrain of the streets of California. There is now an international organization for street lugers, called the International Gravity Sports Association (IGSA), which was formed in 1996. Street lugers are capable of speeds of eighty miles per hour (130 kph). It is now considered a competitive sport and is part of the X-Games in the United States, where extreme sports are presented in Olympic style.

▲ The luge is a long craft (up to eight feet/2.5 m long). The rider or "pilot" operates it from a lying-down position. The pilots steer by "leaning" from side to side, which shifts their weight slightly.

Gear for the Pilot

The pilot wears a leather suit and a full-face motorcycle helmet that is adapted to allow the rider to have good vision from his or her lying-down position.

The one-piece leather suit has extra padding in the seat and elbows, and a plastic pad is added to protect the spine. The pilot also wears thick leather gloves.

Equipment

A street luge (bought or made)

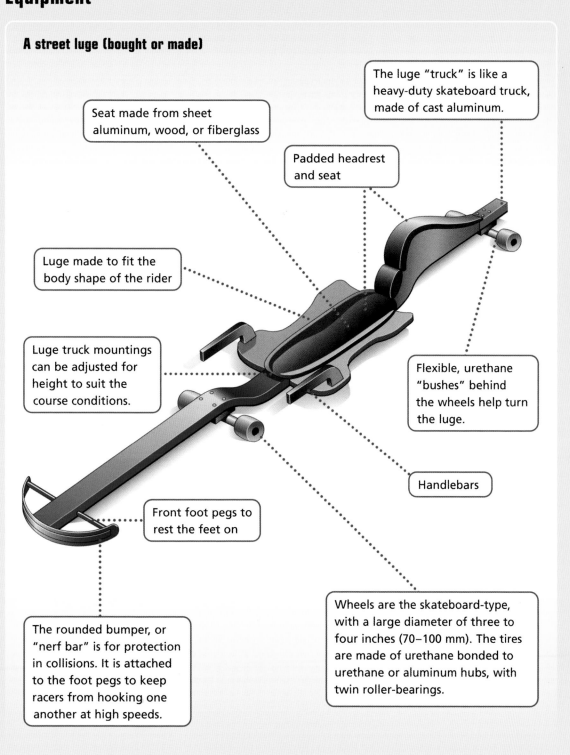

The luge "truck" is like a heavy-duty skateboard truck, made of cast aluminum.

Seat made from sheet aluminum, wood, or fiberglass

Padded headrest and seat

Luge made to fit the body shape of the rider

Luge truck mountings can be adjusted for height to suit the course conditions.

Flexible, urethane "bushes" behind the wheels help turn the luge.

Handlebars

Front foot pegs to rest the feet on

The rounded bumper, or "nerf bar" is for protection in collisions. It is attached to the foot pegs to keep racers from hooking one another at high speeds.

Wheels are the skateboard-type, with a large diameter of three to four inches (70–100 mm). The tires are made of urethane bonded to urethane or aluminum hubs, with twin roller-bearings.

WHY DO IT?

Jim, a street luger from San Francisco

Luging gives you such a thrill! The adrenaline rush is awesome!

It's so dangerous!

Josie, Jim's mother

Street luging began on city streets, but the public are seriously afraid of the danger and see it as a cheap-thrill ride. Sure it can be dangerous, but I wear protective clothing so I don't get hurt badly if I crash. I get out of the way if anything comes behind me.
I stay out of the way of people. Because it's illegal, we've been forced off the streets and into parking garages. It's so unfair that cyclists are allowed on the roads and street lugers are not.

The Lingo

amped – to be filled with the adrenaline rush that comes with street luging

chucking bales – hitting the hay bales (that line the tracks as barriers) hard enough to move them

drop a hill – to ride a luge course

flame – caused by luge wheels catching fire as a result of high speed

flesh wing – extending an arm for steering during a run

hysteria – uncontrolled wobble during a run

junkyard – luges left on the track after a multiple-luge collision

6

Street luging races have become extremely popular. They are held on streets closed to traffic, or on private roads. Street lugers can reach speeds of eighty miles per hour (130 kph).

Lugers need thick soles on their boots because they brake with their feet.

Snowboarding

Snowboarding combines the grace of surfing with the spin and jump techniques of skateboarding.

Developed in the 1960s, snowboarding started here in the United States, when people experimented with the idea of "surfing on the snow." The sport developed very quickly, and the early basic boards changed as specialized designs were made to meet the demands of different competitions.

In 1994, snowboarding was declared an official Olympic sport.

Equipment

A Board

The basic board is like a skateboard without wheels. The average-sized board is about five feet long by ten inches wide (150 x 25 cm).

There are two types: one for freeriding downhill, the other for freestyle boarding, which includes "riding the pipe" and doing the jumps that make great television stunts.

HOW TO GET STARTED

- Strap your front foot onto the board. This places your toes over one edge and your heel against the other.
- Push off with your free back foot as if you were propelling a skateboard.

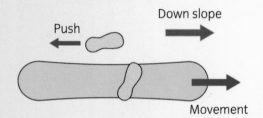

- When you are ready to start going downhill, put your back foot in its strap and allow yourself to drift down the mountain.
- Face forward, keeping your hands in front of you and your knees bent.

- Try not to catch the edge of the board too sharply in the snow, because this will make you crash.
- To turn, lean forward or backward and from side to side, using the toe edge and the heel edge of the board for speed control.

- To stop, turn until the board is across the slope, and skid to a stop.

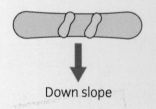

Bindings

Your boots are attached to the board with bindings. These have base plates and straps that can be tightened with a ratchet. Unlike ski bindings they are not supposed to release when you crash. If you want to skate or glide along flat areas you have to disconnect one binding and push with the free foot.

For advanced boarders, the base plate is replaced with a set of rails, which allow your foot to be in direct contact with the board. This gives a better feel and a faster response.

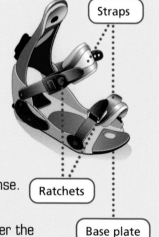

Boots

These are usually chunky, thick boots made in either the latest hi-tech materials or leather. They have rounded, blunt toes, which make your feet look small. You will usually require one size larger than your normal shoe size.

WHY DO IT?

I've been snowboarding since I was a little kid — I was so small when I started, there wasn't even a board small enough for me.

Shaun White, a California snowboarder, was called "Future Boy" when he turned pro at only thirteen years old.

Dr. Bill Smith is a specialist in sports injuries.

"Do you see many broken legs as a result of snowboarding?"

I don't see that many. Upper limb injuries are more common. They are the result of falling onto an outstretched arm, so I see more wrist fractures than anything else. Methods are constantly being developed to reduce this risk. Many snowboarding injuries occur to people who have not bothered to get good instruction, which is never a wise move.

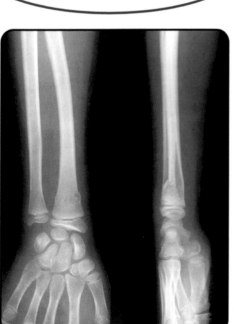

◀ Wrist fractures are the most common snowboarding injury.

The Lingo

air – any aerial trick

boned – this describes the style element of a trick, when the rider's arms or legs are stretched or straightened for flair

crail air – the rear hand grabs the toe edge in front of the front foot, while the rear leg is boned (stretched)

fakie – riding backward

halfpipe – this is similar to a skateboard halfpipe. It is made of snow and is generally built on a slope. It is about 650 feet (200 m) long, of varying width, and has a flat bottom that curves up to the vertical sides. Spins, flips, and board grabs are performed in a halfpipe.

▲ Attempting a spin in a halfpipe

hucker – a rider who throws himself or herself wildly through the air and does not land on his or her feet

nose – front tip of the snowboard

ollie – method of getting into the air without a jump by first lifting the front foot, then lifting the back foot as you spring off the tail

rock and roll – boarder rides up a wall, balances on the top edge of a halfpipe, and then reenters the pipe smoothly without turning at all

rolling down the windows – when a rider is off balance and waves his or her arms in the air while trying to recover

11

Aggressive Skating

Aggressive skating is not about aggression. The skating may be aggressive, but the people doing it and the attitude are not. It is all about fun. It is skating for yourself and helping those around you to have a great time too. Skaters can reach amazing speeds, which makes this one of the most dangerous extreme sports. It is recognized as a competitive sport in the X-Games.

▲ The world-record speed for aggressive skating is more than 62 miles per hour (100 kph).

In-line skates have a brake ▶ pad behind the wheels.

Skating Gear

Most skaters just wear a T-shirt and baggy pants. A well-fitting helmet is an essential safety precaution. Elbow and knee pads and fingerless leather gloves with wrist braces can be worn for extra protection.

Equipment

The Skates

An expert should measure your feet to make sure the skates fit correctly.

Sit down to have the length, arch, and width of both feet measured, then stand up and take note if the measurements change. A noticeable change could mean you tend to turn one or both feet in, and you may need a specially made insole. Both feet should feel comfortable and snug in the skates.

The Lining

Some skates come with a thin lining like a sock; others have thick, comfy liners inside. The lining should be well made and even throughout, with extra padding in the toes.

Lace-up liners offer greater support and fit better than the regular stitched liners.

The Wheels

The ideal wheel shape is a wide wheel with a flat surface. This gives the largest and most stable base for tricks. A durometer is an instrument that measures the wheel hardness. Hard wheels are long-lasting and reduce the wheel's grip on the ground for easier slides and grinds. The heavier you are, the harder the wheels have to be, so they won't wear down too quickly. Softer wheels cushion the impact if you want to do jumps and stair rides.

Most aggressive skate wheels have small, hard cores, or none at all. The core keeps the wheel strong and tough enough to stand up to the pounding it takes from street and trick skating.

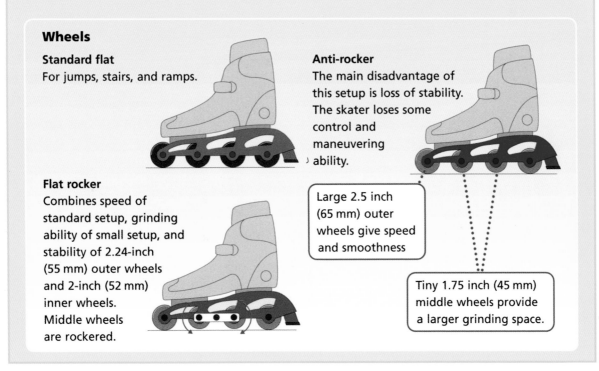

Wheels

Standard flat
For jumps, stairs, and ramps.

Flat rocker
Combines speed of standard setup, grinding ability of small setup, and stability of 2.24-inch (55 mm) outer wheels and 2-inch (52 mm) inner wheels. Middle wheels are rockered.

Anti-rocker
The main disadvantage of this setup is loss of stability. The skater loses some control and maneuvering ability.

Large 2.5 inch (65 mm) outer wheels give speed and smoothness

Tiny 1.75 inch (45 mm) middle wheels provide a larger grinding space.

Stair-riding is a favorite stunt. ▶

WAS IT WORTH IT?

Mrs. Lawson is fifty years old. She is having a cast put on her hand.

How did that happen, Mrs. Lawson?

It happened when I was aggressive skating.

Were you going fast?

Doctor

Mrs. Lawson

It's a little embarrassing. You see, I wasn't moving at all. When you're standing still, it's pretty difficult to balance.

The Lingo

alley-oop – a move in which you turn one way while rotating the other way

armor – your pads... wear them with pride

bump – stair-riding, as in "let's go bump some stairs"

bunny – a new skater who is always holding on to things for support

coping – the metal bar that runs horizontally across the top of a ramp for easier grinding

dropping in – entering a ramp from the top

grind – when you jump onto something and skid down it on the sides of your skates

grommet – a young skater

late tricks – a spinning trick done just before you land

pump – what you do to gain speed on ramps. It involves bending and extending your legs and pumping your arms to help you keep moving.

vert – a ramp that curves up to a vertical wall

wax – scraping wax onto curbs or rails for easier grinding

▲ Competitions can involve performing amazing spins, jumps, and tricks.

Boogie Boarding

Boogie boarding is a water sport, often taken up as an introduction to surfing.

In Australia, many children are given their first boogie board at an early age to use as a swimming aid, instead of water wings. Australians who spend a lot of time in the water become highly skilled at what can be an extremely dangerous sport.

Equipment

A Boogie Board

Compared to the cost of most sports equipment, boogie boards are relatively cheap.

The length of the board depends on your height. The taller the rider, the longer the board should be. It should come up to your belly button. If you ride smaller waves, the board can be a little longer, but if you ride big waves, the board should be shorter.

The width of the nose influences the water displacement, speed, and maneuverability of the board.

Velcro straps

Plastic cord

Channels provide extra hold especially in steep, fast waves.

Nose

Boogie boarding is very dependent on the weather. It is possible to boogie board on low waves, but the best waves are right before and after a storm. So winter is really the best time for boarding – if the air and water are warm enough, of course!

◀ It feels great to catch a wave.

Boogie Boarding Gear

Trunks or a swimming suit

Flippers or fins (optional)

A short-bladed fin gives a quicker thrust motion. Fins are used to increase speed and make it easier to get into the right position for a wave.

Fin tether cord to tie the fins to your feet

Life jacket is always important to stay safe

Wetsuit for professional boarders or for people who want to board all year long. It must be skintight. It helps keep you warm and provides buoyancy, like a life jacket.

Maintenance

The top of the board should be waxed. Make sure the bottom of the board has no cuts or gouges, since boogie boarding requires a smooth surface.

SO WHAT DO YOU DO?

- The idea of boogie boarding is to ride the waves.
- Lie down on your stomach on the board, kicking and holding on to it while riding a wave.
- The goal is to get up as high as you can on the face of the wave, stay in the wave, and – as it crashes – perform tricks and spins.
- When experienced, you can try riding the waves standing up – and maybe even doing backflips.

Basic Tricks

Paddling

Paddle alternately with your hands and legs to conserve energy.

Keep your body relaxed, preferably with both hands gripping the nose of the board.

Your waist should be on the tail of the board and your elbows in a relaxed position.

Kick your feet with an even rhythm.

Balancing is not as easy as it looks. The important thing is to get your body weight in the right position.

Wiping Out

"Wiping out" means falling off your board while riding a wave. Know your limits and only ride the waves you feel ready for.

- Hold your breath.
- Stay calm and try not to fight the wave too hard.
- If you wipe out over a reef, roll into a ball with your hands and arms over your head to protect it if you hit the bottom.

Landing

Be aware of how deep or shallow the waves are breaking, since this will determine how you should land. If the waves are deep, dive deep and push through the back of the wave. If they are shallow and you are in an uncontrollable situation, spread your body out so that you make a shallower landing.

Don't fall on the shore side of your board if you can help it.

WHY DO IT?

You need to watch the water. When you come to a "rapid," there is a drop of about a yard (meter). When waves come up, you see this steep drop. You go down and up and catch the wave. It feels great.

Dana, a boogie boarder

The Lingo

backhand surfing – riding with one's back to the wave

black hole – a group of teenage kids who don't even go into the water

Donald Duck – a beginner trying to walk in new fins – and taking lots of falls

double up – two waves that join

snapped – getting hurt by a big wave

sponge attack – splashing the boarder next to you by slapping a finned foot onto the surface of the water

washing machine – being spun around under water a few times before you reach the surface again

wet brain – an uncoordinated boarder

zooed out – when the water is too full of people

▼ Don't forget to hold your breath when you wipe out.

Sport Climbing

Sport climbing is the most rapidly growing type of climbing. It has two advantages over traditional rock climbing: it is not as expensive, and more people are able to find somewhere to try it. You can sport climb on a wall or rock, as well as on a mountain.

Cliffs are often used for sport climbing, which is fun and often competitive. The winner in a match would be the fastest or the best climber. In sport climbing, you can complete many different routes in a single day. This sport continues to lure new recruits all the time.

So What Do You Do?

Sport climbing can be done anywhere that has fixed bolts or anchor points already in place – in gyms, on outdoor crags, and on walls specifically built for competition climbing. It involves high-intensity, difficult climbing on fairly short, preplanned routes.

Climbers follow the route and clip their ropes into fixed bolts during their ascent. Because the bolts and holds are already in place, the emphasis is on the physical skills involved in making the moves, rather than simply finding the route to the top.

Difficult moves are what count, so climbers don't waste time and energy carrying equipment or placing extra gear for protection. The main aim is to be quick and light. Unlike in traditional climbing,

▲ Expert sport climbers need to be quick, light on their feet, and have good balance.

falling is normal. You expect to fall while figuring out a difficult move. The climber's energy and time are spent on solving these kinds of challenges.

Climbers are often attracted to indoor gyms with climbing walls because they offer a place to practice and train even in bad weather, or at night. The holds are changed frequently, so there are always new problems to attempt. Sport climbing standards are improving all the time.

We may see sport climbing as an Olympic sport in the future.

Equipment

Rope
Hi-tech climbing rope, usually .35 to .45 of an inch (nine or eleven mm) thick, is strong but flexible and is made of nylon, or the new synthetic fiber, Kevlar.

Padded safety harnesses are light, streamlined, and padded to cushion repeated falls. They are worn around the waist and thighs.

Rock (or climbing) shoes have thin soles, which are made of high-friction rubber. They are a tight fit so the climber can feel every tiny bump underfoot.

Helmet
A helmet should be worn when climbing outdoors. It will protect your head from loose, falling rocks.

Quickdraw sets are preattached carabiner clip-and-sling sets that are used to link a rope to the fixed bolts.

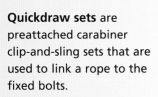
Quickdraw

Carabiner

Techniques

The middle of the rope is clipped into an anchor point at the top of climb.

Both ends of the rope hang down to the bottom of the climb.

The climber clips onto one end and starts to climb.

The partner is clipped to the anchor point at the bottom, and takes in slack in the other end of the rope as the climber ascends.

The climber is always protected with a tight rope, so any fall will be short.

▲ Top roping is an excellent way for climbers to push themselves to their limits. Outdoor crag and cliff climbers often use a top rope for extra protection.

Carabiner
A strong steel link with a screw-gate that opens it.

Chalk is useful for keeping hands dry on difficult moves that have small or delicate holds.

The Lingo

flash – climbing a route on the first attempt without falling or hanging on the rope. The climber has been given information about what moves to make.

on-sight flash – when a climber has completed the entire route in the first attempt without falling and without knowing anything about the route beforehand

pinkpoint – the successful climb of a route where all the quickdraw carabiners are preplaced. All the climber has to do for protection is clip the rope into each carabiner

protection – climbers give themselves protection by clipping the rope attached

WHY DO IT?

Arturo is a student and avid sport climber. He is being interviewed with his friends while recovering from a serious fall.

"So is this it, Arturo? Will you give up climbing now?"

I was extremely shaken up for a few weeks. I was lead-climbing when it happened. I like to take calculated risks. When I ace a tricky move or reach the top, I get an incredible rush.

Arturo

"You still haven't answered my question."

"What do your friends think about all this?"

No, I won't give up, but I'll be more moderate and err on the side of caution.

Ask them.

to their harness onto the bolts hammered into the wall

redpoint – this describes the successful climb of a route that the climber has attempted many times

top roping – ascending a route while clipped on to a safety rope fastened to the top of the wall. If you start to fall, the top rope immediately checks your fall.

▶ Some sport climbers take up the challenge of ice climbing.

"Don't you worry about him injuring himself?"

"How about you, Anish? Should he give up?"

I'm upset that Arturo hurt himself, but I admire his positive attitude. I am going to go climbing with him when he's recovered.

Michal

Normal climbing with a rope is fairly safe. I just think Arturo pushed himself beyond his limits. He's definitely learned from this experience.

Anish

I do worry about him, but this time he knew he had gone beyond his own ability. He's decided not to take unnecessary risks anymore.

I worry about him because he's much more casual about the risks than I would be. Although, that's probably what makes him good at the sport.

Michal

"Would you prefer it if he didn't do it?"

Sara

No, because then he wouldn't be Arturo.

Bungee Jumping

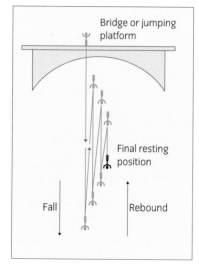

◀ This breathtaking bungee jump is using the New Zealand system, where you end up hanging upside down.

Bridge or jumping platform

Final resting position

Fall

Rebound

In the Past

According to one legend, bungee jumping evolved from an incident that took place on an island in the South Pacific. The story says that a woman, trying to run away from her husband, tied a vine around her ankle and threw herself out of a tall tree. Her husband had followed her up into the tree and leaned out to catch her as she fell. He fell to his death while she was saved by the vine. The men of the village were impressed by her jump and began to hold competitions, and vine jumping became a local tradition. In 1979, a movie of this unusual custom inspired the Oxford Dangerous Sports Club to try similar jumps, using stretchy rubber cords that are often called "bungee cords." The sport of bungee jumping was born!

▲ It all began with vine jumping!

Present

Bungee jumping is popular today all over the world.

Extreme forms of bungee jumping involve leaping from helicopters and balloons in order to extend the distance of the freefall.

In 1988, brothers John and Peter Kockelman founded the first bungee jumping company in the United States. The brothers, who are both engineers, wrote many of the safety rules and regulations that keep people safe in the sport today.

In the Future

There are plans to arrange bungee competitions. These will involve accuracy tests, in which the jumper has to grasp specific targets on the ground or in the water. A variety of acrobatic moves and tricks are also being incorporated into the jumps. High-divers often can perform amazing tricks during bungee jumps.

The Lingo

bungee rope – elastic rope with a core of rubber cords and a braided nylon outer casing

freefall – the downward plunge before the cord runs out and "catches," and starts to stretch and slow the fall

Equipment

In addition to a bridge, high building, or crane cage from which to fall, you will need:

Harness

Means of attachment, e.g. carabiners

Safety line

Cord

▲ Bungee jumping from a crane, using the American system of two harnesses. The chest harness helps you to turn the right way up when you have stopped bouncing.

rebound – the upward movement that starts when the stretched cord starts to contract

static freefall – when the jumper "hovers," weightless, at the top of the bounce

The Two Main Systems

The European/New Zealand system uses a single rubber cord attached to a harness around the ankles, over protective padding. The thickness of the cord is selected is based on the weight of the jumper. A second safety line provides added security. This system "catches" sooner, and gives less freefall.

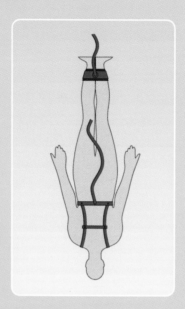

The American system uses two harnesses, one around the waist or shoulders, and one around the ankles. Extra cords are added according to the jumper's weight: one cord for each fifty pounds (twenty-three kg). There are two anchor points, for extra security. This system gives more freefall and greater deceleration.

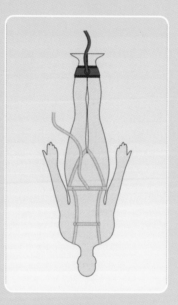

In both systems, energy is stored in the elastic cords, which stretch until they stop the freefall. Then the cords contract and propel the jumper back up. After a few freefalls and bounces, the jumper comes to a rest.

The person's weight is written on their hand to help with double checking.

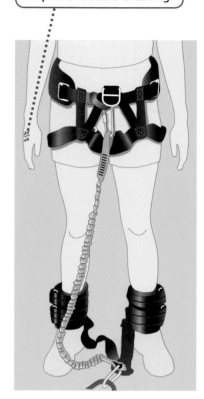

▲ Most companies use a leg harness to take most of the weight, and a body harness or a climbing harness for backup. The body harness also makes the ride more comfortable if you have to be hauled back up.

WHY DO IT?

This was my first time. I thought the worst part of it would be hanging upside down at the bottom, but actually that wasn't so bad. Standing on the top before you jump, however, is another story. If I'd been alone I probably would have chickened out.

"Is it dangerous?"

Matthew

It's supposed to be safe. My greatest fear was that the rope would snap. I've heard of a couple of minor mishaps. A friend of mine had two very red eyes just from the blood rush due to deceleration.

"Why do you do it, Matthew?"

I do it for the sheer thrill of it. It is just amazing, and every jump is just as exciting as the first.

"Are you going to try it?"

Laura

No way! I like watching, but you won't catch me leaping from a platform 160 feet (fifty m) above the ground. Like most extreme sports, you can get hurt if something goes wrong.

Quidditch and Other Fantasy Sports

Quidditch

This is the most extreme of the dangerous sports covered in this book. Like the others, the players, gear, and technique all play their part. However, for quidditch, one extra ingredient is required – a little bit of magic.

▼ In quidditch, the seeker has to catch the golden snitch.

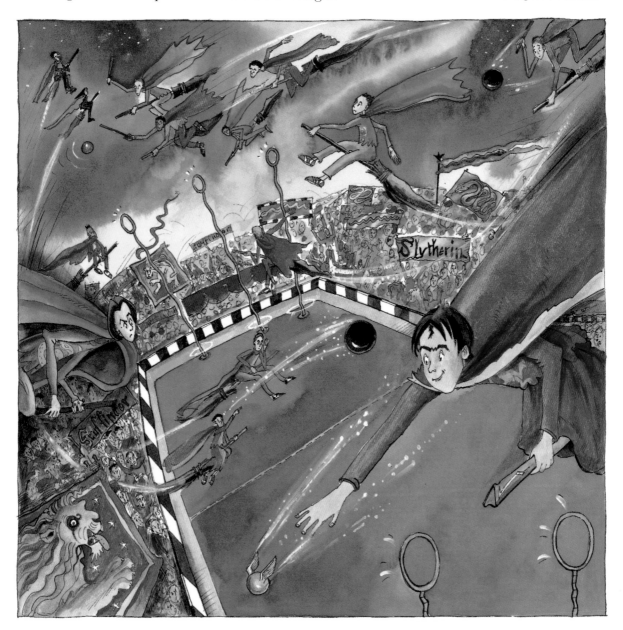

So for those who think practice makes perfect, forget it! When it comes to quidditch, you won't make it into the air unless you have some inherited wizardry, (even if, like Harry Potter, you don't discover it until you are eleven years old).

Equipment

A broomstick

Magical talent. If you find you can do strange magical things without even trying, visit "Quality Quidditch Supplies" in Diagon Alley for the complete range of broomsticks.

How to Play

Quidditch is played in the air.

It is played on, or rather above, a field surrounded by hundreds of seats raised on stands so that people at the back can see.

At either end of the field are three golden poles with hoops on the end about sixty feet (eighteen m) high.

Each side has seven players:

> three chasers
> one keeper
> one seeker
> two beaters

There are four balls:

> *the quaffle*
> a large, red, soccer-sized ball
> *two bludgers*
> black and slightly smaller than the quaffle
> Watch out – these can be dangerous!
> *the snitch*
> walnut-sized and bright gold with
> silver wings

The chasers from each team throw the quaffle to each other, trying to put it through the other team's hoops to score a goal and win ten points for their team.

The keeper flies around the hoops, keeping the opposing team from scoring.

The bludgers whiz around and try to knock the players off their brooms.

The beaters protect their side from the bludgers and try to knock them toward the opposing team.

The seeker's job is to catch the golden snitch. This is difficult because the snitch is so fast, it is hard to see. The seeker has to weave in and out of all the other players and try to catch the snitch before the other team's seeker gets to it.

The game ends when the golden snitch is caught. The seeker who catches it wins 150 points for their team.

Rumor has it that the longest quidditch game in history lasted three months!

Flamingo Croquet

Croquet is a fiercely competitive game when played by ordinary people on a lawn with metal hoops, wooden balls, and mallets. However, when the Queen of Hearts invited Alice in Wonderland to play, flamingos were used as mallets, hedgehogs as balls, and the playing-card gardeners had to bend themselves into hoops. If the Queen was not allowed to win, she would shriek, "Off with his head."

◄ In the story of *Alice in Wonderland*, the Queen of Hearts enjoyed an argumentative game of flamingo croquet.

Books for Further Reading

The Adventure Sports Directory, published by
Central Books

Over the Edge: A Regular Guy's Odyssey in Extreme Sports
by Michael Bane, published by Victor Gollancz

The Strange Adventures of the Dangerous Sports Club
by Martin Lyster, published by The Do Not Press

Street Luge Survival Guide by Darren Lott,
published by Gravity Publishing

Some Fun Websites

www.shaunwhite.com

> Go visit Shaun's very own webpage – his
> brother updates it regularly!

http://www.ncdsa.com/gen_tab1.asp?CatID=29&
IPSearchOnPostID=167454

> This official site for the Northern California
> Skateboarding Association has information
> about street luging gear and competitions, and a
> great question-and-answer section.

www.lanikai.k12.hi.us/WATER/RECREATION/
boogie.htm

> Learn all about boogie boarding, and other
> exciting water sports.

WARNING – DANGER

These sports are known as
dangerous or extreme sports
precisely because they can be
dangerous. So if you are
seriously considering taking
up one of these sports, the
essential things you should
do are:

- Find out about getting the
  right training.

- Contact the official
  organization for that sport
  and make sure that the
  organization itself is
  affiliated to a respected body
  with a good safety record.

- Make sure you have all the
  right equipment to try the
  sport with the minimum
  of risk.

- Figure out and write down a
  contact number so that
  someone can be called if you
  need any kind of help.

Index